THIS BOOK BELONGS TO:

_____

_____

_____

A

NAME:

ADDRESS:

HOME:

WORK:

MOBILE:

SOCIAL MEDIA:

BIRTHDAY:

- -

NAME:

ADDRESS:

HOME:

WORK:

MOBILE:

SOCIAL MEDIA:

BIRTHDAY:

- -

NAME:

ADDRESS:

HOME:

WORK:

MOBILE:

SOCIAL MEDIA:

BIRTHDAY:

NAME:

ADDRESS:

HOME:

WORK:

MOBILE:

SOCIAL MEDIA:

BIRTHDAY:

- -

NAME:

ADDRESS:

HOME:

WORK:

MOBILE:

SOCIAL MEDIA:

BIRTHDAY:

- -

NAME:

ADDRESS:

HOME:

WORK:

MOBILE:

SOCIAL MEDIA:

BIRTHDAY:

A

NAME:
ADDRESS:

HOME:
WORK:
MOBILE:
SOCIAL MEDIA:
BIRTHDAY:

- -

NAME:
ADDRESS:

HOME:
WORK:
MOBILE:
SOCIAL MEDIA:
BIRTHDAY:

- -

NAME:
ADDRESS:

HOME:
WORK:
MOBILE:
SOCIAL MEDIA:
BIRTHDAY:

NAME: _____

ADDRESS: _____

_____

HOME: _____

WORK: _____

MOBILE: _____

SOCIAL MEDIA: _____

BIRTHDAY: _____

- -

NAME: _____

ADDRESS: _____

_____

HOME: _____

WORK: _____

MOBILE: _____

SOCIAL MEDIA: _____

BIRTHDAY: _____

- -

NAME: _____

ADDRESS: _____

_____

HOME: _____

WORK: _____

MOBILE: _____

SOCIAL MEDIA: _____

BIRTHDAY: _____

B

NAME:

ADDRESS:

HOME:

WORK:

MOBILE:

SOCIAL MEDIA:

BIRTHDAY:

NAME:

ADDRESS:

HOME:

WORK:

MOBILE:

SOCIAL MEDIA:

BIRTHDAY:

NAME:

ADDRESS:

HOME:

WORK:

MOBILE:

SOCIAL MEDIA:

BIRTHDAY:

NAME:

ADDRESS:

HOME:

WORK:

MOBILE:

SOCIAL MEDIA:

BIRTHDAY:

- -

NAME:

ADDRESS:

HOME:

WORK:

MOBILE:

SOCIAL MEDIA:

BIRTHDAY:

- -

NAME:

ADDRESS:

HOME:

WORK:

MOBILE:

SOCIAL MEDIA:

BIRTHDAY:

B

NAME: _____

ADDRESS: _____

_____

HOME: _____

WORK: _____

MOBILE: _____

SOCIAL MEDIA: _____

BIRTHDAY: _____

- -

NAME: _____

ADDRESS: _____

_____

HOME: _____

WORK: _____

MOBILE: _____

SOCIAL MEDIA: _____

BIRTHDAY: _____

- -

NAME: _____

ADDRESS: _____

_____

HOME: _____

WORK: _____

MOBILE: _____

SOCIAL MEDIA: _____

BIRTHDAY: _____

NAME: _____

ADDRESS: _____

_____

HOME: _____

WORK: _____

MOBILE: _____

SOCIAL MEDIA: _____

BIRTHDAY: _____

- -

NAME: _____

ADDRESS: _____

_____

HOME: _____

WORK: _____

MOBILE: _____

SOCIAL MEDIA: _____

BIRTHDAY: _____

- -

NAME: _____

ADDRESS: _____

_____

HOME: _____

WORK: _____

MOBILE: _____

SOCIAL MEDIA: _____

BIRTHDAY: _____

C

NAME:

ADDRESS:

HOME:

WORK:

MOBILE:

SOCIAL MEDIA:

BIRTHDAY:

NAME:

ADDRESS:

HOME:

WORK:

MOBILE:

SOCIAL MEDIA:

BIRTHDAY:

NAME:

ADDRESS:

HOME:

WORK:

MOBILE:

SOCIAL MEDIA:

BIRTHDAY:

C

NAME:

ADDRESS:

HOME:

WORK:

MOBILE:

SOCIAL MEDIA:

BIRTHDAY:

- -

NAME:

ADDRESS:

HOME:

WORK:

MOBILE:

SOCIAL MEDIA:

BIRTHDAY:

- -

NAME:

ADDRESS:

HOME:

WORK:

MOBILE:

SOCIAL MEDIA:

BIRTHDAY:

C

NAME: _____

ADDRESS: _____

_____

HOME: _____

WORK: _____

MOBILE: _____

SOCIAL MEDIA: _____

BIRTHDAY: _____

- -

NAME: _____

ADDRESS: _____

_____

HOME: _____

WORK: _____

MOBILE: _____

SOCIAL MEDIA: _____

BIRTHDAY: _____

- -

NAME: _____

ADDRESS: _____

_____

HOME: _____

WORK: _____

MOBILE: _____

SOCIAL MEDIA: _____

BIRTHDAY: _____

NAME:

ADDRESS:

HOME:

WORK:

MOBILE:

SOCIAL MEDIA:

BIRTHDAY:

- -

NAME:

ADDRESS:

HOME:

WORK:

MOBILE:

SOCIAL MEDIA:

BIRTHDAY:

- -

NAME:

ADDRESS:

HOME:

WORK:

MOBILE:

SOCIAL MEDIA:

BIRTHDAY:

D

NAME: _____

ADDRESS: _____

_____

HOME: _____

WORK: _____

MOBILE: _____

SOCIAL MEDIA: _____

BIRTHDAY: _____

- -

NAME: _____

ADDRESS: _____

_____

HOME: _____

WORK: _____

MOBILE: _____

SOCIAL MEDIA: _____

BIRTHDAY: _____

- -

NAME: _____

ADDRESS: _____

_____

HOME: _____

WORK: _____

MOBILE: _____

SOCIAL MEDIA: _____

BIRTHDAY: _____

NAME:

ADDRESS:

HOME:

WORK:

MOBILE:

SOCIAL MEDIA:

BIRTHDAY:

- -

NAME:

ADDRESS:

HOME:

WORK:

MOBILE:

SOCIAL MEDIA:

BIRTHDAY:

- -

NAME:

ADDRESS:

HOME:

WORK:

MOBILE:

SOCIAL MEDIA:

BIRTHDAY:

D

NAME: _____

ADDRESS: _____

_____

HOME: _____

WORK: _____

MOBILE: _____

SOCIAL MEDIA: _____

BIRTHDAY: _____

- -

NAME: _____

ADDRESS: _____

_____

HOME: _____

WORK: _____

MOBILE: _____

SOCIAL MEDIA: _____

BIRTHDAY: _____

- -

NAME: _____

ADDRESS: _____

_____

HOME: _____

WORK: _____

MOBILE: _____

SOCIAL MEDIA: _____

BIRTHDAY: _____

D

NAME:

ADDRESS:

HOME:

WORK:

MOBILE:

SOCIAL MEDIA:

BIRTHDAY:

NAME:

ADDRESS:

HOME:

WORK:

MOBILE:

SOCIAL MEDIA:

BIRTHDAY:

NAME:

ADDRESS:

HOME:

WORK:

MOBILE:

SOCIAL MEDIA:

BIRTHDAY:

E

NAME:

ADDRESS:

HOME:

WORK:

MOBILE:

SOCIAL MEDIA:

BIRTHDAY:

NAME:

ADDRESS:

HOME:

WORK:

MOBILE:

SOCIAL MEDIA:

BIRTHDAY:

NAME:

ADDRESS:

HOME:

WORK:

MOBILE:

SOCIAL MEDIA:

BIRTHDAY:

NAME: _____

ADDRESS: _____

_____

HOME: _____

WORK: _____

MOBILE: _____

SOCIAL MEDIA: _____

BIRTHDAY: _____

- -

NAME: _____

ADDRESS: _____

_____

HOME: _____

WORK: _____

MOBILE: _____

SOCIAL MEDIA: _____

BIRTHDAY: _____

- -

NAME: _____

ADDRESS: _____

_____

HOME: _____

WORK: _____

MOBILE: _____

SOCIAL MEDIA: _____

BIRTHDAY: _____

E

NAME:

ADDRESS:

HOME:

WORK:

MOBILE:

SOCIAL MEDIA:

BIRTHDAY:

- -

NAME:

ADDRESS:

HOME:

WORK:

MOBILE:

SOCIAL MEDIA:

BIRTHDAY:

- -

NAME:

ADDRESS:

HOME:

WORK:

MOBILE:

SOCIAL MEDIA:

BIRTHDAY:

NAME:

ADDRESS:

HOME:

WORK:

MOBILE:

SOCIAL MEDIA:

BIRTHDAY:

- -

NAME:

ADDRESS:

HOME:

WORK:

MOBILE:

SOCIAL MEDIA:

BIRTHDAY:

- -

NAME:

ADDRESS:

HOME:

WORK:

MOBILE:

SOCIAL MEDIA:

BIRTHDAY:

F

NAME: _____

ADDRESS: _____

_____

HOME: _____

WORK: _____

MOBILE: _____

SOCIAL MEDIA: _____

BIRTHDAY: _____

- -

NAME: _____

ADDRESS: _____

_____

HOME: _____

WORK: _____

MOBILE: _____

SOCIAL MEDIA: _____

BIRTHDAY: _____

- -

NAME: _____

ADDRESS: _____

_____

HOME: _____

WORK: _____

MOBILE: _____

SOCIAL MEDIA: _____

BIRTHDAY: _____

NAME:

ADDRESS:

HOME:

WORK:

MOBILE:

SOCIAL MEDIA:

BIRTHDAY:

- -

NAME:

ADDRESS:

HOME:

WORK:

MOBILE:

SOCIAL MEDIA:

BIRTHDAY:

- -

NAME:

ADDRESS:

HOME:

WORK:

MOBILE:

SOCIAL MEDIA:

BIRTHDAY:

F

NAME: _____

ADDRESS: _____

_____

HOME: _____

WORK: _____

MOBILE: _____

SOCIAL MEDIA: _____

BIRTHDAY: _____

- -

NAME: _____

ADDRESS: _____

_____

HOME: _____

WORK: _____

MOBILE: _____

SOCIAL MEDIA: _____

BIRTHDAY: _____

- -

NAME: _____

ADDRESS: _____

_____

HOME: _____

WORK: _____

MOBILE: _____

SOCIAL MEDIA: _____

BIRTHDAY: _____

NAME: _____

ADDRESS: _____

_____

HOME: _____

WORK: _____

MOBILE: _____

SOCIAL MEDIA: _____

BIRTHDAY: _____

- -

NAME: _____

ADDRESS: _____

_____

HOME: _____

WORK: _____

MOBILE: _____

SOCIAL MEDIA: _____

BIRTHDAY: _____

- -

NAME: _____

ADDRESS: _____

_____

HOME: _____

WORK: _____

MOBILE: _____

SOCIAL MEDIA: _____

BIRTHDAY: _____

G

NAME: _____

ADDRESS: _____

_____

HOME: _____

WORK: _____

MOBILE: _____

SOCIAL MEDIA: _____

BIRTHDAY: _____

- -

NAME: _____

ADDRESS: _____

_____

HOME: _____

WORK: _____

MOBILE: _____

SOCIAL MEDIA: _____

BIRTHDAY: _____

- -

NAME: _____

ADDRESS: _____

_____

HOME: _____

WORK: _____

MOBILE: _____

SOCIAL MEDIA: _____

BIRTHDAY: _____

NAME:

ADDRESS:

HOME:

WORK:

MOBILE:

SOCIAL MEDIA:

BIRTHDAY:

- -

NAME:

ADDRESS:

HOME:

WORK:

MOBILE:

SOCIAL MEDIA:

BIRTHDAY:

- -

NAME:

ADDRESS:

HOME:

WORK:

MOBILE:

SOCIAL MEDIA:

BIRTHDAY:

G

NAME:

ADDRESS:

HOME:

WORK:

MOBILE:

SOCIAL MEDIA:

BIRTHDAY:

- -

NAME:

ADDRESS:

HOME:

WORK:

MOBILE:

SOCIAL MEDIA:

BIRTHDAY:

- -

NAME:

ADDRESS:

HOME:

WORK:

MOBILE:

SOCIAL MEDIA:

BIRTHDAY:

NAME:

ADDRESS:

HOME:

WORK:

MOBILE:

SOCIAL MEDIA:

BIRTHDAY:

NAME:

ADDRESS:

HOME:

WORK:

MOBILE:

SOCIAL MEDIA:

BIRTHDAY:

NAME:

ADDRESS:

HOME:

WORK:

MOBILE:

SOCIAL MEDIA:

BIRTHDAY:

H

NAME:
ADDRESS:

HOME:
WORK:
MOBILE:
SOCIAL MEDIA:
BIRTHDAY:

- -

NAME:
ADDRESS:

HOME:
WORK:
MOBILE:
SOCIAL MEDIA:
BIRTHDAY:

- -

NAME:
ADDRESS:

HOME:
WORK:
MOBILE:
SOCIAL MEDIA:
BIRTHDAY:

NAME:

ADDRESS:

HOME:

WORK:

MOBILE:

SOCIAL MEDIA:

BIRTHDAY:

- -

NAME:

ADDRESS:

HOME:

WORK:

MOBILE:

SOCIAL MEDIA:

BIRTHDAY:

- -

NAME:

ADDRESS:

HOME:

WORK:

MOBILE:

SOCIAL MEDIA:

BIRTHDAY:

H

NAME: _____

ADDRESS: _____

_____

HOME: _____

WORK: _____

MOBILE: _____

SOCIAL MEDIA: _____

BIRTHDAY: _____

- -

NAME: _____

ADDRESS: _____

_____

HOME: _____

WORK: _____

MOBILE: _____

SOCIAL MEDIA: _____

BIRTHDAY: _____

- -

NAME: _____

ADDRESS: _____

_____

HOME: _____

WORK: _____

MOBILE: _____

SOCIAL MEDIA: _____

BIRTHDAY: _____

NAME:

ADDRESS:

HOME:

WORK:

MOBILE:

SOCIAL MEDIA:

BIRTHDAY:

- -

NAME:

ADDRESS:

HOME:

WORK:

MOBILE:

SOCIAL MEDIA:

BIRTHDAY:

- -

NAME:

ADDRESS:

HOME:

WORK:

MOBILE:

SOCIAL MEDIA:

BIRTHDAY:

I

NAME: _____

ADDRESS: _____

_____

HOME: _____

WORK: _____

MOBILE: _____

SOCIAL MEDIA: _____

BIRTHDAY: _____

NAME: _____

ADDRESS: _____

_____

HOME: _____

WORK: _____

MOBILE: _____

SOCIAL MEDIA: _____

BIRTHDAY: _____

NAME: _____

ADDRESS: _____

_____

HOME: _____

WORK: _____

MOBILE: _____

SOCIAL MEDIA: _____

BIRTHDAY: _____

NAME:

ADDRESS:

HOME:

WORK:

MOBILE:

SOCIAL MEDIA:

BIRTHDAY:

- -

NAME:

ADDRESS:

HOME:

WORK:

MOBILE:

SOCIAL MEDIA:

BIRTHDAY:

- -

NAME:

ADDRESS:

HOME:

WORK:

MOBILE:

SOCIAL MEDIA:

BIRTHDAY:

NAME: _____
ADDRESS: _____

_____
HOME: _____
WORK: _____
MOBILE: _____
SOCIAL MEDIA: _____
BIRTHDAY: _____

- -

NAME: _____
ADDRESS: _____

_____
HOME: _____
WORK: _____
MOBILE: _____
SOCIAL MEDIA: _____
BIRTHDAY: _____

- -

NAME: _____
ADDRESS: _____

_____
HOME: _____
WORK: _____
MOBILE: _____
SOCIAL MEDIA: _____
BIRTHDAY: _____

NAME: _____
ADDRESS: _____
_____
HOME: _____
WORK: _____
MOBILE: _____
SOCIAL MEDIA: _____
BIRTHDAY: _____

NAME: _____
ADDRESS: _____
_____
HOME: _____
WORK: _____
MOBILE: _____
SOCIAL MEDIA: _____
BIRTHDAY: _____

NAME: _____
ADDRESS: _____
_____
HOME: _____
WORK: _____
MOBILE: _____
SOCIAL MEDIA: _____
BIRTHDAY: _____

J

NAME:

ADDRESS:

HOME:

WORK:

MOBILE:

SOCIAL MEDIA:

BIRTHDAY:

NAME:

ADDRESS:

HOME:

WORK:

MOBILE:

SOCIAL MEDIA:

BIRTHDAY:

NAME:

ADDRESS:

HOME:

WORK:

MOBILE:

SOCIAL MEDIA:

BIRTHDAY:

J

NAME:
ADDRESS:

HOME:
WORK:
MOBILE:
SOCIAL MEDIA:
BIRTHDAY:

- -

NAME:
ADDRESS:

HOME:
WORK:
MOBILE:
SOCIAL MEDIA:
BIRTHDAY:

- -

NAME:
ADDRESS:

HOME:
WORK:
MOBILE:
SOCIAL MEDIA:
BIRTHDAY:

J

NAME:

ADDRESS:

HOME:

WORK:

MOBILE:

SOCIAL MEDIA:

BIRTHDAY:

NAME:

ADDRESS:

HOME:

WORK:

MOBILE:

SOCIAL MEDIA:

BIRTHDAY:

NAME:

ADDRESS:

HOME:

WORK:

MOBILE:

SOCIAL MEDIA:

BIRTHDAY:

NAME: _____

ADDRESS: _____

_____

HOME: _____

WORK: _____

MOBILE: _____

SOCIAL MEDIA: _____

BIRTHDAY: _____

- -

NAME: _____

ADDRESS: _____

_____

HOME: _____

WORK: _____

MOBILE: _____

SOCIAL MEDIA: _____

BIRTHDAY: _____

- -

NAME: _____

ADDRESS: _____

_____

HOME: _____

WORK: _____

MOBILE: _____

SOCIAL MEDIA: _____

BIRTHDAY: _____

K

NAME:

ADDRESS:

HOME:

WORK:

MOBILE:

SOCIAL MEDIA:

BIRTHDAY:

NAME:

ADDRESS:

HOME:

WORK:

MOBILE:

SOCIAL MEDIA:

BIRTHDAY:

NAME:

ADDRESS:

HOME:

WORK:

MOBILE:

SOCIAL MEDIA:

BIRTHDAY:

K

NAME:

ADDRESS:

HOME:

WORK:

MOBILE:

SOCIAL MEDIA:

BIRTHDAY:

NAME:

ADDRESS:

HOME:

WORK:

MOBILE:

SOCIAL MEDIA:

BIRTHDAY:

NAME:

ADDRESS:

HOME:

WORK:

MOBILE:

SOCIAL MEDIA:

BIRTHDAY:

K

NAME:

ADDRESS:

HOME:

WORK:

MOBILE:

SOCIAL MEDIA:

BIRTHDAY:

- -

NAME:

ADDRESS:

HOME:

WORK:

MOBILE:

SOCIAL MEDIA:

BIRTHDAY:

- -

NAME:

ADDRESS:

HOME:

WORK:

MOBILE:

SOCIAL MEDIA:

BIRTHDAY:

NAME:

ADDRESS:

HOME:

WORK:

MOBILE:

SOCIAL MEDIA:

BIRTHDAY:

- -

NAME:

ADDRESS:

HOME:

WORK:

MOBILE:

SOCIAL MEDIA:

BIRTHDAY:

- -

NAME:

ADDRESS:

HOME:

WORK:

MOBILE:

SOCIAL MEDIA:

BIRTHDAY:

L

NAME: _____
ADDRESS: _____
_____
HOME: _____
WORK: _____
MOBILE: _____
SOCIAL MEDIA: _____
BIRTHDAY: _____

NAME: _____
ADDRESS: _____
_____
HOME: _____
WORK: _____
MOBILE: _____
SOCIAL MEDIA: _____
BIRTHDAY: _____

NAME: _____
ADDRESS: _____
_____
HOME: _____
WORK: _____
MOBILE: _____
SOCIAL MEDIA: _____
BIRTHDAY: _____

NAME:

ADDRESS:

HOME:

WORK:

MOBILE:

SOCIAL MEDIA:

BIRTHDAY:

- -

NAME:

ADDRESS:

HOME:

WORK:

MOBILE:

SOCIAL MEDIA:

BIRTHDAY:

- -

NAME:

ADDRESS:

HOME:

WORK:

MOBILE:

SOCIAL MEDIA:

BIRTHDAY:

L

NAME:

ADDRESS:

HOME:

WORK:

MOBILE:

SOCIAL MEDIA:

BIRTHDAY:

NAME:

ADDRESS:

HOME:

WORK:

MOBILE:

SOCIAL MEDIA:

BIRTHDAY:

NAME:

ADDRESS:

HOME:

WORK:

MOBILE:

SOCIAL MEDIA:

BIRTHDAY:

NAME: _____

ADDRESS: _____

_____

HOME: _____

WORK: _____

MOBILE: _____

SOCIAL MEDIA: _____

BIRTHDAY: _____

NAME: _____

ADDRESS: _____

_____

HOME: _____

WORK: _____

MOBILE: _____

SOCIAL MEDIA: _____

BIRTHDAY: _____

NAME: _____

ADDRESS: _____

_____

HOME: _____

WORK: _____

MOBILE: _____

SOCIAL MEDIA: _____

BIRTHDAY: _____

M

NAME:

ADDRESS:

HOME:

WORK:

MOBILE:

SOCIAL MEDIA:

BIRTHDAY:

- -

NAME:

ADDRESS:

HOME:

WORK:

MOBILE:

SOCIAL MEDIA:

BIRTHDAY:

- -

NAME:

ADDRESS:

HOME:

WORK:

MOBILE:

SOCIAL MEDIA:

BIRTHDAY:

NAME:

ADDRESS:

HOME:

WORK:

MOBILE:

SOCIAL MEDIA:

BIRTHDAY:

NAME:

ADDRESS:

HOME:

WORK:

MOBILE:

SOCIAL MEDIA:

BIRTHDAY:

NAME:

ADDRESS:

HOME:

WORK:

MOBILE:

SOCIAL MEDIA:

BIRTHDAY:

M

NAME:

ADDRESS:

HOME:

WORK:

MOBILE:

SOCIAL MEDIA:

BIRTHDAY:

- -

NAME:

ADDRESS:

HOME:

WORK:

MOBILE:

SOCIAL MEDIA:

BIRTHDAY:

- -

NAME:

ADDRESS:

HOME:

WORK:

MOBILE:

SOCIAL MEDIA:

BIRTHDAY:

NAME:

ADDRESS:

HOME:

WORK:

MOBILE:

SOCIAL MEDIA:

BIRTHDAY:

- -

NAME:

ADDRESS:

HOME:

WORK:

MOBILE:

SOCIAL MEDIA:

BIRTHDAY:

- -

NAME:

ADDRESS:

HOME:

WORK:

MOBILE:

SOCIAL MEDIA:

BIRTHDAY:

N

NAME: _____

ADDRESS: _____

_____

HOME: _____

WORK: _____

MOBILE: _____

SOCIAL MEDIA: _____

BIRTHDAY: _____

- -

NAME: _____

ADDRESS: _____

_____

HOME: _____

WORK: _____

MOBILE: _____

SOCIAL MEDIA: _____

BIRTHDAY: _____

- -

NAME: _____

ADDRESS: _____

_____

HOME: _____

WORK: _____

MOBILE: _____

SOCIAL MEDIA: _____

BIRTHDAY: _____

NAME: _____

ADDRESS: _____

_____

HOME: _____

WORK: _____

MOBILE: _____

SOCIAL MEDIA: _____

BIRTHDAY: _____

- -

NAME: _____

ADDRESS: _____

_____

HOME: _____

WORK: _____

MOBILE: _____

SOCIAL MEDIA: _____

BIRTHDAY: _____

- -

NAME: _____

ADDRESS: _____

_____

HOME: _____

WORK: _____

MOBILE: _____

SOCIAL MEDIA: _____

BIRTHDAY: _____

N

NAME:

ADDRESS:

HOME:

WORK:

MOBILE:

SOCIAL MEDIA:

BIRTHDAY:

NAME:

ADDRESS:

HOME:

WORK:

MOBILE:

SOCIAL MEDIA:

BIRTHDAY:

NAME:

ADDRESS:

HOME:

WORK:

MOBILE:

SOCIAL MEDIA:

BIRTHDAY:

NAME: _____

ADDRESS: _____

_____

HOME: _____

WORK: _____

MOBILE: _____

SOCIAL MEDIA: _____

BIRTHDAY: _____

NAME: _____

ADDRESS: _____

_____

HOME: _____

WORK: _____

MOBILE: _____

SOCIAL MEDIA: _____

BIRTHDAY: _____

NAME: _____

ADDRESS: _____

_____

HOME: _____

WORK: _____

MOBILE: _____

SOCIAL MEDIA: _____

BIRTHDAY: _____

NAME:

ADDRESS:

HOME:

WORK:

MOBILE:

SOCIAL MEDIA:

BIRTHDAY:

NAME:

ADDRESS:

HOME:

WORK:

MOBILE:

SOCIAL MEDIA:

BIRTHDAY:

NAME:

ADDRESS:

HOME:

WORK:

MOBILE:

SOCIAL MEDIA:

BIRTHDAY:

NAME:

ADDRESS:

HOME:

WORK:

MOBILE:

SOCIAL MEDIA:

BIRTHDAY:

- -

NAME:

ADDRESS:

HOME:

WORK:

MOBILE:

SOCIAL MEDIA:

BIRTHDAY:

- -

NAME:

ADDRESS:

HOME:

WORK:

MOBILE:

SOCIAL MEDIA:

BIRTHDAY:

NAME:
ADDRESS:

HOME:
WORK:
MOBILE:
SOCIAL MEDIA:
BIRTHDAY:

NAME:
ADDRESS:

HOME:
WORK:
MOBILE:
SOCIAL MEDIA:
BIRTHDAY:

NAME:
ADDRESS:

HOME:
WORK:
MOBILE:
SOCIAL MEDIA:
BIRTHDAY:

NAME:

ADDRESS:

HOME:

WORK:

MOBILE:

SOCIAL MEDIA:

BIRTHDAY:

- -

NAME:

ADDRESS:

HOME:

WORK:

MOBILE:

SOCIAL MEDIA:

BIRTHDAY:

- -

NAME:

ADDRESS:

HOME:

WORK:

MOBILE:

SOCIAL MEDIA:

BIRTHDAY:

P

NAME:

ADDRESS:

HOME:

WORK:

MOBILE:

SOCIAL MEDIA:

BIRTHDAY:

NAME:

ADDRESS:

HOME:

WORK:

MOBILE:

SOCIAL MEDIA:

BIRTHDAY:

NAME:

ADDRESS:

HOME:

WORK:

MOBILE:

SOCIAL MEDIA:

BIRTHDAY:

NAME: _____
ADDRESS: _____
_____
HOME: _____
WORK: _____
MOBILE: _____
SOCIAL MEDIA: _____
BIRTHDAY: _____

- -

NAME: _____
ADDRESS: _____
_____
HOME: _____
WORK: _____
MOBILE: _____
SOCIAL MEDIA: _____
BIRTHDAY: _____

- -

NAME: _____
ADDRESS: _____
_____
HOME: _____
WORK: _____
MOBILE: _____
SOCIAL MEDIA: _____
BIRTHDAY: _____

P

NAME: _____

ADDRESS: _____

_____

HOME: _____

WORK: _____

MOBILE: _____

SOCIAL MEDIA: _____

BIRTHDAY: _____

- -

NAME: _____

ADDRESS: _____

_____

HOME: _____

WORK: _____

MOBILE: _____

SOCIAL MEDIA: _____

BIRTHDAY: _____

- -

NAME: _____

ADDRESS: _____

_____

HOME: _____

WORK: _____

MOBILE: _____

SOCIAL MEDIA: _____

BIRTHDAY: _____

NAME: _____

ADDRESS: _____

_____

HOME: _____

WORK: _____

MOBILE: _____

SOCIAL MEDIA: _____

BIRTHDAY: _____

- -

NAME: _____

ADDRESS: _____

_____

HOME: _____

WORK: _____

MOBILE: _____

SOCIAL MEDIA: _____

BIRTHDAY: _____

- -

NAME: _____

ADDRESS: _____

_____

HOME: _____

WORK: _____

MOBILE: _____

SOCIAL MEDIA: _____

BIRTHDAY: _____

Q

NAME: _____

ADDRESS: _____

_____

HOME: _____

WORK: _____

MOBILE: _____

SOCIAL MEDIA: _____

BIRTHDAY: _____

- -

NAME: _____

ADDRESS: _____

_____

HOME: _____

WORK: _____

MOBILE: _____

SOCIAL MEDIA: _____

BIRTHDAY: _____

- -

NAME: _____

ADDRESS: _____

_____

HOME: _____

WORK: _____

MOBILE: _____

SOCIAL MEDIA: _____

BIRTHDAY: _____

NAME: _____

ADDRESS: _____

_____

HOME: _____

WORK: _____

MOBILE: _____

SOCIAL MEDIA: _____

BIRTHDAY: _____

- -

NAME: _____

ADDRESS: _____

_____

HOME: _____

WORK: _____

MOBILE: _____

SOCIAL MEDIA: _____

BIRTHDAY: _____

- -

NAME: _____

ADDRESS: _____

_____

HOME: _____

WORK: _____

MOBILE: _____

SOCIAL MEDIA: _____

BIRTHDAY: _____

Q

NAME: _____

ADDRESS: _____
_____

HOME: _____

WORK: _____

MOBILE: _____

SOCIAL MEDIA: _____

BIRTHDAY: _____

- -

NAME: _____

ADDRESS: _____
_____

HOME: _____

WORK: _____

MOBILE: _____

SOCIAL MEDIA: _____

BIRTHDAY: _____

- -

NAME: _____

ADDRESS: _____
_____

HOME: _____

WORK: _____

MOBILE: _____

SOCIAL MEDIA: _____

BIRTHDAY: _____

NAME:

ADDRESS:

HOME:

WORK:

MOBILE:

SOCIAL MEDIA:

BIRTHDAY:

- -

NAME:

ADDRESS:

HOME:

WORK:

MOBILE:

SOCIAL MEDIA:

BIRTHDAY:

- -

NAME:

ADDRESS:

HOME:

WORK:

MOBILE:

SOCIAL MEDIA:

BIRTHDAY:

R

NAME:

ADDRESS:

HOME:

WORK:

MOBILE:

SOCIAL MEDIA:

BIRTHDAY:

- -

NAME:

ADDRESS:

HOME:

WORK:

MOBILE:

SOCIAL MEDIA:

BIRTHDAY:

- -

NAME:

ADDRESS:

HOME:

WORK:

MOBILE:

SOCIAL MEDIA:

BIRTHDAY:

NAME: _____
ADDRESS: _____
_____
HOME: _____
WORK: _____
MOBILE: _____
SOCIAL MEDIA: _____
BIRTHDAY: _____

- -

NAME: _____
ADDRESS: _____
_____
HOME: _____
WORK: _____
MOBILE: _____
SOCIAL MEDIA: _____
BIRTHDAY: _____

- -

NAME: _____
ADDRESS: _____
_____
HOME: _____
WORK: _____
MOBILE: _____
SOCIAL MEDIA: _____
BIRTHDAY: _____

R

NAME:

ADDRESS:

HOME:

WORK:

MOBILE:

SOCIAL MEDIA:

BIRTHDAY:

NAME:

ADDRESS:

HOME:

WORK:

MOBILE:

SOCIAL MEDIA:

BIRTHDAY:

NAME:

ADDRESS:

HOME:

WORK:

MOBILE:

SOCIAL MEDIA:

BIRTHDAY:

NAME:

ADDRESS:

HOME:

WORK:

MOBILE:

SOCIAL MEDIA:

BIRTHDAY:

NAME:

ADDRESS:

HOME:

WORK:

MOBILE:

SOCIAL MEDIA:

BIRTHDAY:

NAME:

ADDRESS:

HOME:

WORK:

MOBILE:

SOCIAL MEDIA:

BIRTHDAY:

S

NAME: _____

ADDRESS: _____

_____

HOME: _____

WORK: _____

MOBILE: _____

SOCIAL MEDIA: _____

BIRTHDAY: _____

- -

NAME: _____

ADDRESS: _____

_____

HOME: _____

WORK: _____

MOBILE: _____

SOCIAL MEDIA: _____

BIRTHDAY: _____

- -

NAME: _____

ADDRESS: _____

_____

HOME: _____

WORK: _____

MOBILE: _____

SOCIAL MEDIA: _____

BIRTHDAY: _____

NAME:

ADDRESS:

HOME:

WORK:

MOBILE:

SOCIAL MEDIA:

BIRTHDAY:

- -

NAME:

ADDRESS:

HOME:

WORK:

MOBILE:

SOCIAL MEDIA:

BIRTHDAY:

- -

NAME:

ADDRESS:

HOME:

WORK:

MOBILE:

SOCIAL MEDIA:

BIRTHDAY:

S

NAME:

ADDRESS:

HOME:

WORK:

MOBILE:

SOCIAL MEDIA:

BIRTHDAY:

- -

NAME:

ADDRESS:

HOME:

WORK:

MOBILE:

SOCIAL MEDIA:

BIRTHDAY:

- -

NAME:

ADDRESS:

HOME:

WORK:

MOBILE:

SOCIAL MEDIA:

BIRTHDAY:

NAME:

ADDRESS:

HOME:

WORK:

MOBILE:

SOCIAL MEDIA:

BIRTHDAY:

NAME:

ADDRESS:

HOME:

WORK:

MOBILE:

SOCIAL MEDIA:

BIRTHDAY:

NAME:

ADDRESS:

HOME:

WORK:

MOBILE:

SOCIAL MEDIA:

BIRTHDAY:

T

NAME:

ADDRESS:

HOME:

WORK:

MOBILE:

SOCIAL MEDIA:

BIRTHDAY:

- -

NAME:

ADDRESS:

HOME:

WORK:

MOBILE:

SOCIAL MEDIA:

BIRTHDAY:

- -

NAME:

ADDRESS:

HOME:

WORK:

MOBILE:

SOCIAL MEDIA:

BIRTHDAY:

NAME: _____
ADDRESS: _____
_____

HOME: _____
WORK: _____
MOBILE: _____
SOCIAL MEDIA: _____
BIRTHDAY: _____

- -

NAME: _____
ADDRESS: _____
_____

HOME: _____
WORK: _____
MOBILE: _____
SOCIAL MEDIA: _____
BIRTHDAY: _____

- -

NAME: _____
ADDRESS: _____
_____

HOME: _____
WORK: _____
MOBILE: _____
SOCIAL MEDIA: _____
BIRTHDAY: _____

T

NAME: _____

ADDRESS: _____

_____

HOME: _____

WORK: _____

MOBILE: _____

SOCIAL MEDIA: _____

BIRTHDAY: _____

- -

NAME: _____

ADDRESS: _____

_____

HOME: _____

WORK: _____

MOBILE: _____

SOCIAL MEDIA: _____

BIRTHDAY: _____

- -

NAME: _____

ADDRESS: _____

_____

HOME: _____

WORK: _____

MOBILE: _____

SOCIAL MEDIA: _____

BIRTHDAY: _____

NAME:

ADDRESS:

HOME:

WORK:

MOBILE:

SOCIAL MEDIA:

BIRTHDAY:

- -

NAME:

ADDRESS:

HOME:

WORK:

MOBILE:

SOCIAL MEDIA:

BIRTHDAY:

- -

NAME:

ADDRESS:

HOME:

WORK:

MOBILE:

SOCIAL MEDIA:

BIRTHDAY:

U

NAME:

ADDRESS:

HOME:

WORK:

MOBILE:

SOCIAL MEDIA:

BIRTHDAY:

- -

NAME:

ADDRESS:

HOME:

WORK:

MOBILE:

SOCIAL MEDIA:

BIRTHDAY:

- -

NAME:

ADDRESS:

HOME:

WORK:

MOBILE:

SOCIAL MEDIA:

BIRTHDAY:

U

NAME:

ADDRESS:

HOME:

WORK:

MOBILE:

SOCIAL MEDIA:

BIRTHDAY:

- -

NAME:

ADDRESS:

HOME:

WORK:

MOBILE:

SOCIAL MEDIA:

BIRTHDAY:

- -

NAME:

ADDRESS:

HOME:

WORK:

MOBILE:

SOCIAL MEDIA:

BIRTHDAY:

U

NAME:

ADDRESS:

HOME:

WORK:

MOBILE:

SOCIAL MEDIA:

BIRTHDAY:

- -

NAME:

ADDRESS:

HOME:

WORK:

MOBILE:

SOCIAL MEDIA:

BIRTHDAY:

- -

NAME:

ADDRESS:

HOME:

WORK:

MOBILE:

SOCIAL MEDIA:

BIRTHDAY:

NAME:

ADDRESS:

HOME:

WORK:

MOBILE:

SOCIAL MEDIA:

BIRTHDAY:

NAME:

ADDRESS:

HOME:

WORK:

MOBILE:

SOCIAL MEDIA:

BIRTHDAY:

NAME:

ADDRESS:

HOME:

WORK:

MOBILE:

SOCIAL MEDIA:

BIRTHDAY:

V

NAME:

ADDRESS:

HOME:

WORK:

MOBILE:

SOCIAL MEDIA:

BIRTHDAY:

- -

NAME:

ADDRESS:

HOME:

WORK:

MOBILE:

SOCIAL MEDIA:

BIRTHDAY:

- -

NAME:

ADDRESS:

HOME:

WORK:

MOBILE:

SOCIAL MEDIA:

BIRTHDAY:

NAME:

ADDRESS:

HOME:

WORK:

MOBILE:

SOCIAL MEDIA:

BIRTHDAY:

- -

NAME:

ADDRESS:

HOME:

WORK:

MOBILE:

SOCIAL MEDIA:

BIRTHDAY:

- -

NAME:

ADDRESS:

HOME:

WORK:

MOBILE:

SOCIAL MEDIA:

BIRTHDAY:

V

NAME:

ADDRESS:

HOME:

WORK:

MOBILE:

SOCIAL MEDIA:

BIRTHDAY:

NAME:

ADDRESS:

HOME:

WORK:

MOBILE:

SOCIAL MEDIA:

BIRTHDAY:

NAME:

ADDRESS:

HOME:

WORK:

MOBILE:

SOCIAL MEDIA:

BIRTHDAY:

V

NAME:

ADDRESS:

HOME:

WORK:

MOBILE:

SOCIAL MEDIA:

BIRTHDAY:

- -

NAME:

ADDRESS:

HOME:

WORK:

MOBILE:

SOCIAL MEDIA:

BIRTHDAY:

- -

NAME:

ADDRESS:

HOME:

WORK:

MOBILE:

SOCIAL MEDIA:

BIRTHDAY:

W

NAME:

ADDRESS:

HOME:

WORK:

MOBILE:

SOCIAL MEDIA:

BIRTHDAY:

NAME:

ADDRESS:

HOME:

WORK:

MOBILE:

SOCIAL MEDIA:

BIRTHDAY:

NAME:

ADDRESS:

HOME:

WORK:

MOBILE:

SOCIAL MEDIA:

BIRTHDAY:

NAME:

ADDRESS:

HOME:

WORK:

MOBILE:

SOCIAL MEDIA:

BIRTHDAY:

- -

NAME:

ADDRESS:

HOME:

WORK:

MOBILE:

SOCIAL MEDIA:

BIRTHDAY:

- -

NAME:

ADDRESS:

HOME:

WORK:

MOBILE:

SOCIAL MEDIA:

BIRTHDAY:

W

NAME: _____

ADDRESS: _____

_____

HOME: _____

WORK: _____

MOBILE: _____

SOCIAL MEDIA: _____

BIRTHDAY: _____

- -

NAME: _____

ADDRESS: _____

_____

HOME: _____

WORK: _____

MOBILE: _____

SOCIAL MEDIA: _____

BIRTHDAY: _____

- -

NAME: _____

ADDRESS: _____

_____

HOME: _____

WORK: _____

MOBILE: _____

SOCIAL MEDIA: _____

BIRTHDAY: _____

NAME:

ADDRESS:

HOME:

WORK:

MOBILE:

SOCIAL MEDIA:

BIRTHDAY:

- -

NAME:

ADDRESS:

HOME:

WORK:

MOBILE:

SOCIAL MEDIA:

BIRTHDAY:

- -

NAME:

ADDRESS:

HOME:

WORK:

MOBILE:

SOCIAL MEDIA:

BIRTHDAY:

X

NAME: _____

ADDRESS: _____

_____

HOME: _____

WORK: _____

MOBILE: _____

SOCIAL MEDIA: _____

BIRTHDAY: _____

- -

NAME: _____

ADDRESS: _____

_____

HOME: _____

WORK: _____

MOBILE: _____

SOCIAL MEDIA: _____

BIRTHDAY: _____

- -

NAME: _____

ADDRESS: _____

_____

HOME: _____

WORK: _____

MOBILE: _____

SOCIAL MEDIA: _____

BIRTHDAY: _____

X

NAME:

ADDRESS:

HOME:

WORK:

MOBILE:

SOCIAL MEDIA:

BIRTHDAY:

- -

NAME:

ADDRESS:

HOME:

WORK:

MOBILE:

SOCIAL MEDIA:

BIRTHDAY:

- -

NAME:

ADDRESS:

HOME:

WORK:

MOBILE:

SOCIAL MEDIA:

BIRTHDAY:

X

NAME: _____

ADDRESS: _____

_____

HOME: _____

WORK: _____

MOBILE: _____

SOCIAL MEDIA: _____

BIRTHDAY: _____

- -

NAME: _____

ADDRESS: _____

_____

HOME: _____

WORK: _____

MOBILE: _____

SOCIAL MEDIA: _____

BIRTHDAY: _____

- -

NAME: _____

ADDRESS: _____

_____

HOME: _____

WORK: _____

MOBILE: _____

SOCIAL MEDIA: _____

BIRTHDAY: _____

NAME:

ADDRESS:

HOME:

WORK:

MOBILE:

SOCIAL MEDIA:

BIRTHDAY:

- -

NAME:

ADDRESS:

HOME:

WORK:

MOBILE:

SOCIAL MEDIA:

BIRTHDAY:

- -

NAME:

ADDRESS:

HOME:

WORK:

MOBILE:

SOCIAL MEDIA:

BIRTHDAY:

Y

NAME:

ADDRESS:

HOME:

WORK:

MOBILE:

SOCIAL MEDIA:

BIRTHDAY:

- -

NAME:

ADDRESS:

HOME:

WORK:

MOBILE:

SOCIAL MEDIA:

BIRTHDAY:

- -

NAME:

ADDRESS:

HOME:

WORK:

MOBILE:

SOCIAL MEDIA:

BIRTHDAY:

Y

NAME:
ADDRESS:

HOME:
WORK:
MOBILE:
SOCIAL MEDIA:
BIRTHDAY:

- -

NAME:
ADDRESS:

HOME:
WORK:
MOBILE:
SOCIAL MEDIA:
BIRTHDAY:

- -

NAME:
ADDRESS:

HOME:
WORK:
MOBILE:
SOCIAL MEDIA:
BIRTHDAY:

Y

NAME:

ADDRESS:

HOME:

WORK:

MOBILE:

SOCIAL MEDIA:

BIRTHDAY:

- -

NAME:

ADDRESS:

HOME:

WORK:

MOBILE:

SOCIAL MEDIA:

BIRTHDAY:

- -

NAME:

ADDRESS:

HOME:

WORK:

MOBILE:

SOCIAL MEDIA:

BIRTHDAY:

NAME:

ADDRESS:

HOME:

WORK:

MOBILE:

SOCIAL MEDIA:

BIRTHDAY:

- -

NAME:

ADDRESS:

HOME:

WORK:

MOBILE:

SOCIAL MEDIA:

BIRTHDAY:

- -

NAME:

ADDRESS:

HOME:

WORK:

MOBILE:

SOCIAL MEDIA:

BIRTHDAY:

Z

NAME: _____

ADDRESS: _____

_____

HOME: _____

WORK: _____

MOBILE: _____

SOCIAL MEDIA: _____

BIRTHDAY: _____

- -

NAME: _____

ADDRESS: _____

_____

HOME: _____

WORK: _____

MOBILE: _____

SOCIAL MEDIA: _____

BIRTHDAY: _____

- -

NAME: _____

ADDRESS: _____

_____

HOME: _____

WORK: _____

MOBILE: _____

SOCIAL MEDIA: _____

BIRTHDAY: _____

NAME: _____

ADDRESS: _____

_____

HOME: _____

WORK: _____

MOBILE: _____

SOCIAL MEDIA: _____

BIRTHDAY: _____

- -

NAME: _____

ADDRESS: _____

_____

HOME: _____

WORK: _____

MOBILE: _____

SOCIAL MEDIA: _____

BIRTHDAY: _____

- -

NAME: _____

ADDRESS: _____

_____

HOME: _____

WORK: _____

MOBILE: _____

SOCIAL MEDIA: _____

BIRTHDAY: _____

Z

NAME: _____

ADDRESS: _____

_____

HOME: _____

WORK: _____

MOBILE: _____

SOCIAL MEDIA: _____

BIRTHDAY: _____

- -

NAME: _____

ADDRESS: _____

_____

HOME: _____

WORK: _____

MOBILE: _____

SOCIAL MEDIA: _____

BIRTHDAY: _____

- -

NAME: _____

ADDRESS: _____

_____

HOME: _____

WORK: _____

MOBILE: _____

SOCIAL MEDIA: _____

BIRTHDAY: _____

NAME:

ADDRESS:

HOME:

WORK:

MOBILE:

SOCIAL MEDIA:

BIRTHDAY:

- -

NAME:

ADDRESS:

HOME:

WORK:

MOBILE:

SOCIAL MEDIA:

BIRTHDAY:

- -

NAME:

ADDRESS:

HOME:

WORK:

MOBILE:

SOCIAL MEDIA:

BIRTHDAY:

Notes

Notes

Notes

Notes

Notes